COULD A TIGER WALK A TIGHTROPE?

Camilla de la Bédoyère
& Aleksei Bitskoff

QEB

Tigers are big, meat-eating cats.

Design: Duck Egg Blue
Editor: Carly Madden
Editorial Director: Victoria Garrard
Art Director: Laura Roberts-Jensen
Publisher: Maxime Boucknooghe

Copyright © QEB Publishing 2016

First published in the United States in 2016 by
Part of the Quarto Group
QEB Publishing
6 Orchard
Lake Forest
CA 92630

www.qed-publishing.co.uk

A CIP record for this book is available from Library of Congress.

ISBN 978 1 60992 944 2

Printed in China

They like to sleep and eat...and then sleep and eat some more!

Imagine if a Bengal tiger came to stay. What would he like to do?

What if a tiger came for dinner?

Tigers eat lots of meat.
One tiger could
gobble down
100 cans
of cat food in one meal.

He wouldn't need to
eat again for **days.**

A tiger would try to hide his food from everyone. Tigers hate to share their food!

What if a tiger joined a karate class?

He could sneak, creep, and leap without making a noise.

In the wild, tigers are stealthy hunters that tiptoe through the jungle in silence.

Their furry paws help to muffle the sound of their footsteps, so their prey never hears them coming.

Would a tiger have fun in a bounce house?

He would love **bouncing...**

...and **pouncing!**

Tigers love to jump into trees, where they lie on branches and watch all the other animals below.

Some tigers can leap 13 feet high.
That's the height of a bounce house.

But look out for those sharp,
curved claws.
There might be a loud...

POP!

Could a tiger walk a tightrope?

Like all cats, a tiger can keep his balance. He wouldn't

fall...

...even if he tried some tricks!

He'd use his...

long **tail** to keep him steady.

A good sense of balance means a tiger can walk on branches.

He can also twist and turn quickly as he runs through his jungle home.

What if a tiger got a haircut?

He would still be stripy!

Tigers have orange fur
with dark stripes, but their
skin is stripy too.

Every tiger has its own **special pattern** of stripes.

A tiger's stripes help him to hide in the long jungle grass, and creep invisibly through the shadows when he hunts.

Could a tiger join a rock band?

He might not pass the audition! Tigers aren't musical, but they are...

loud!

A tiger's **roar** is as loud as an electric guitar, played at *full blast!*

Tigers also growl and hiss but, unlike pet cats, they can't purr.

What if a tiger went to the dentist?

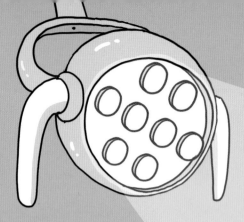

It would take a **brave** dentist to look inside a tiger's mouth!

After eating so much meat, tigers have very...

actual size!

What if a tiger went to a playground?

He would have no trouble

leaping

to the top of a playset...

...but he might get **stuck** there!

Tigers are quick to climb trees, but they forget they aren't so good at getting down.

They have to hug the tree trunk, and shuffle down it backward.

But this tiger could use the slide!

What would a tiger do at the swimming pool?

He would dive right in!

Most cats hate getting wet, but not tigers.
They love water and are great swimmers.

A tiger can swim nearly 4 miles without stopping—that's the same as 120 lengths of a swimming pool!

More about Bengal tigers

Bengal tiger is pointing to the places where he lives. Can you see where you live?

FACT FILE

There are five types of tiger. Bengal tigers, like the one in this book, can grow to 10 feet long.

Tigers hunt at night. A tiger can see in the dark about six times better than a human.

Tigers are the largest members of the cat family.

Tigers like to live alone, so they pee on trees to tell other tigers to stay away!

Tiger cubs are born blind. They don't open their eyes until they are 3 weeks old.

Areas where Bengal tigers live

NORTH AMERICA

PACIFIC OCEAN

SOUTH AMERI

Greetings from Mangrove swamp!

POST CARD

As soon as I got home all the monkeys and birds began to hoot, holler, and shriek. The trees were shaking! So everyone must have been happy to see me, and I was happy to see them. Well, I would have been, but they have all disappeared now. How strange!

Take care of yourself.
Love, Tiger X

SENT BY BENGAL TIGER POST
MANGROVE SWAMP

1ST

The Sharp Family
189 Claw Hill
Stripetown
TX 12345

5148263560809178379